What is Lost

poems by

Yehiel E. Poupko

Finishing Line Press
Georgetown, Kentucky

What is Lost

ACKNOWLEDGMENTS

Publisher: Leah Huete de Maines
Editor: Christen Kincaid
Author Photo: Courtesy of the author
Cover Design: Elizabeth Maines McCleavy

Order online: www.finishinglinepress.com
         also available on amazon.com

Author inquiries and mail orders:
Finishing Line Press
P. O. Box 1626
Georgetown, Kentucky 40324
U. S. A.

Table of Contents

Epilogue

for Tzivia

Prologue

Picnics

For my mother, Hinda Poupko (1924-1983), who introduced me at an early age to poetry, especially the poetry of the Torah.

my mother's room
its windows overlooking the river
and the steel mills of my Pittsburgh childhood
Bessemer furnaces stoked with coke and coal
and iron ore
boats and barges floating up
and down the river

yeshiva school children took day trips
to white hot molten rivers ladled into casts
Pittsburgh is big shouldered we were told
and thought this the original
while picnicking lunches on benches
by the river in the glow of iron coke and coal

and now the mills and furnaces are empty
orange rusty and skeletal against the green
wooded mountains that fall into the river
on whose banks is the room the nurse enters
with bottles and bags and needles and tubes
and pumps filled with molten pouring
into my mother who lies in the bed in the room
whose windows look out on the river
and its skeletons

once a month we picnic for lunch
blessed are You Lord our God
Who in His goodness nourishes the world
in the room by the window on the green wooded
banks of the river our monthly chemo picnic
on the bank by the river my mother's bed
shadowing the mills

After a baby's death

My granddaughter, Chana Tova Poupko (March 1, 2012-June 7, 2014)

before i was
and after i am not
light lustrous
only light
and the One
from beginning
to beginning
i am
as she died
the light gutters
and after i am not

I

Kol Nidrei—All my vows

Note: Kol Nidrei, the inaugural Prayer for the Day of Atonement, seeks forgiveness for unfulfilled vows and commitments.

i am lost
a wandering jew
in Yom Kippur
land of violated promises
failed oaths
unkept vows
alien to me
as Canaan
to Abraham
sin's topography
sculpts all form
of landscape

and who shall
scout the land
for dangerous
outcropping
of rock and craggy sin
soul faults
quaking with offense

wadis rushing
with sin
flooded Noah's Ark
shattered on
secret perfidies
sins and lives drowning

the angel recorder
of sins
faithful custodian
of bones crushed
in falling words
echoing through desert

and canyon
none shall escape
the day of the Lord

Roster

as i
read
read and recite
recite and chant
chant and read
the list
and litany
roster
and all
of my
sins
and a few
not yet
thought
and formed
in fantasy
and deed
i wonder
did You
really
make me
make
and create
create and
form
form and knead
knead and breathe
life and
image
as i
read
and recite

Starlings and pigeons

the other
day
between
shofar blast
and Yom Kippur fast
i saw
the starlings
and pigeons
against
the autumn
heavens
god grey
and fateful
flying
racing
southward
to warm
skies
blue
and godless
o that
i had wings

This is not a poem

this is not a poem
nor a parable
it is a vision
from a sin master
to read
the list and liturgy
for we have sinned
is to report
and record
and then to add
and to reckon
and to balance
the accounts
and close the book
and cast to
the cleansing river waters
but if the reading
flows to chant
and chant to singing
and singing to swaying
then guilt and pain
seek their same
in the embrace
of sin
she said
reclining on one arm
for life
is a breath
and sin
its net
as the holy
gives way
to the good

When the goat escaped

while the goat designated by lot for Azazel...to make expiation with it and to send it off to the wilderness for Azazel. (Lev. 16:10)

when the goat
escaped Temple's altar
climbing desert hills
searching the barren
for green and grass
unwittingly bearing
Israel's sins
red ribboned
by a deftly priest
climbing the precipice
the earth yawns
surprises the grass
munching goat
and a sin or two
bounces down
the hill
as goat's brains spill
on rock and crag
all is forgiven

Matza time

it is
matza time
and killing time
a time
for blood
and doors
to wombs
torn ever
open
as first born
sacrifices
animal
and human
are summoned
to altar cross
and circumcision
as He
passes over
the bloodied
sill and lintel
spare this
one
of foreskin
lost
for another
night and time

Sarah's witness

and having laughed
at the news
of a baby
to be born
to her
withered
with years
she laughed
again mockery
lyrics to laughter
she who doubted
that babe and blood
could again flow
down the hillocks
and lipped ravines
long unpleasured
swelled grotesquely young
lest anyone doubt
God's word
about man
and especially woman
and in His time
when the body
and the hills
brought fruit
she who doubted
was mocked
as she at Him
and word laughed
singing joined
by a chorus
of who else
but those men
for all to hear
by Hagar is Isaac
to Abraham born
and he whose

loins and legs
still covenant bloody
she doubted
saying all lost
for laughter
and life
declaimed
as he often
confronted God
if this babe
of my blood
and white
by your fruitfulness
is born
then laughter
and mockery
earn just claim
at your breast
once shriveled
and nipple black
now full
and pink
pay Him due
so she four score
year and more
with breast and babe
erect nipple
God's witness
milk flows
in the desert
of Sarah's barren
breast offered for
suckling babes
and bared for
many a man
mocked

So Job died old and full of days

crammed and jammed
bursting with days
Job died old and full of days
so full of days
he died
died from days clotted with friends
Eliphaz Bildad and
Zophar
and don't forget Elihu
late but stuffed with wisdom too
friends certain and smug
wiseacres knowing all
everything about this life
except of course the life of Job

so full of days
he died
died from days God awed
the heavenly court and Satan dialogue
travel reports and near endless silence
Lordly Master God knowing all
everything about the creation
except of course the children of Job

so full of days
he died
died from days teeming with nature
treasury of snow hems of oceans
the Venus hind birthing at dawn
the morning stars singing
nature indifferent knowing all
everything about the world
except of course the emptiness of Job
who died old and full of days

II

Several sorrows ago

several sorrows ago
before grief came to echo and voice
and tears to a pulsing spring
several sorrows ago
before the poem
and portrait
dared word meaning
and purpose its bastard child

before each witness
knew silence
and its deafening cadence

before blood coursed with pain
and flesh knew but itself
several sorrows ago
when only the old withered
and we were frozen young

eyes that saw not
ears that heard not

before children died
and life just moved with the sun
several sorrows ago
when God still knew us
and we did not

Ukraine 1919—Epitaph

There are of course there are a number of reference points storehouses of metaphors clever devices literary by which to portray dramatize convey and thereby utterly and with feeling imprint upon the mind and soul of the callous and the ignorant what happened here on that pogrom day how life fled like the bird flushed from the bush how blood ran like red mud in spring creek waters how flesh was crushed and woman eviscerated as so many shtetl backyard chickens on a Friday morn's Sabbath cooking all this and more can be crafted as poets take pen from quiver to bow but having now and just been there which is to say having walked listened seen smelled probed hunted investigated and questioned not a few for the story.

what remains is what will be
and what will be
is not what was
and what was is no more
and what is lost
will not return
and all is as it
was, imagined

Neighbors

got to rush
to bahnhoff
train leaving soon
need to get seat
no time to explain
key under mat
cat food in pantry
see to sill plants
before i return
neighbor dearest
of our children's park
watch these
the tricycle
a few jump ropes
toy trucks
and cars
as i go east
to lebensraum
left Bible
just for you
from Luther
a gift in German
till i return
love
your Jude

Bequest to a Berlin neighbor

before i leave
a few things
for safekeeping
i won't
be coming back

my grandmother's Torah
from which you borrowed
love thy neighbor
as thyself
except
for
me

While i am gone

watch over these
it won't be long
lived here some years
home always waits
ancient homes ever patient
a millennium's worth
your house warming gift
my Yiddish tongue
bastard child
of hoch high deutsch
caressing Torah and Talmud
you sired her
in Luther's grace
watch over these
while i am gone
it won't be long

Walking

we are walking
ever since Eden walking
first on garden grass
and then
promised land
first fruit vineyard
and grain field
on to Roman via
walking to exile
and muddy shtetl lanes
washed away to ghettoes
moving to city pavements
streets and squares
at last to walk
Vienna and Paris
and o Berlin
streets paved
with ash and bone
and many
a jew

Last supper

my last
full day
like any other
sun light
over the dark
prayer to the One
let there
be light
in Torah study
over
and ever
again
His word
I am
for breakfast
Who brings forth
bread from the earth
smuggled through
the wall
and labor
to till
and tend
garden
and factory
uniforms
for the front
by the sweat
of my brow
daily bread
this is
my body
daily broken
for transport
via dolorous stations
to chimney
and cross

So many

once we were many
many even myriads
not just women
children and men
not just madmen
prophets and dreamers
lights to the nations
once we were
many actually
some carpenters
and draymen
peddlers bankers
and Bolsheviks
beggars and poor
tailors and shoemakers
and most of all
the radiant ordinary
many ordinaries
all the lives we sent to smoke
all the lives we died

A census

we count
we matter
counting us
by country
numbered
jew by jew
all pass
beneath their rod
not just Poland's
million three
and some tens
or is that hundreds
of thousands more
jew by jew
Albania's two
barely hundreds
jew by jew
they matter too
by two
our numbers
known
inscribed
reckoned
totaled
and final
to be sure
never
our names
never
our faces

A Psalm for…

what about the man
who did not lie down
in green forest glens
of Treblinka
whose ashes
were not scattered
on streams of water
underneath a tree planted
that yields its fruit
in its season
and whose leaves
do not wither
what about the man
whose children
did not go to ash
and fly away
as the winds
caressed the chimneys

Were you there

"Were you there when I laid the foundations of earth?" (Job 38:4)

were You there
were You there in that place
that death-life place
where man become god
chose and selected
to life to death to death to life
with your Moses-rod
in man's godly hand
to right to left
to life to death
and the earth
not ocean split
and the dry land
became Noah's world
death camp
God you were there in that place

Death camp post

if you find this letter
you are…

if you open this letter
you will know…

if you read this letter
you will become…

God's words
alphabet of ashes
wind scattered
we were unwritten

Höss' house

Rudolph Höss was Commandant of the death camp Auschwitz for three-and-a-half years, beginning May 1, 1940. While Commandant he lived with his wife and children in a well-appointed residence on the grounds.

dolls litter the house
clutter the halls
up the stairs
on the landing
where the air stagnates
toes fingers
all sizes and kinds of limbs
digits and numbered arms
stretching to necks chokered

in one room
and through the house
a Viennese waltz
for all to hear
a two minute egg
enthroned on Meissen
firmly but artfully opened
not cracked
not a bit of loose shell
the yolk dipped with dark
German rye
and Twinings
the Brits
know tea

oh daddy daddy
see you for dinner
bring more toys
from so many countries
wonderful toys
Poland and Russia
so many dolls
and all those

Hungary and Slovakia Czech
who bring you wonderful
Jew toys
just tumbling out
the box cars

Let's do lunch

it could have been
Poles or Lithuanians
Ukrainians too
depending on the village
or perhaps the French
with their paté packed
cornichon calico baskets
set a table for mine enemies
in my presence
waving and smiling
flowering them with early roses
and picnic lunches
from black Slavic earth
breads and sausages
slaking vodka and borscht
kerchiefs colored
against long winter grays
fluttering in the wind
amid butterflies bees
and lily pad beetles
farmers with hoes
and shovels
pitchforks
tree chopping axes
some with hammer
and sickle to boot
joining the late spring outing
by the pond
He leadeth me beside still waters
in the
yea though I walk
through the valley of death's shadow
blessed by the priest
in honor of the village Jews
as the Germans
came to picnic

In season

and when autumn came
the jews
and the fire-bright leaves
the cold-killing wind
drove the leaves
floating fluttering
to the wintered ground
and the people and machines
mostly people
ground and trampled
driven leaves
and spring never came

We were not

where we walked
we left no footprint
earth and grass
ignored us
the heavens rained
on others
all others
trees cast
no shade on us
our shadows went unseen
when the chimneys
knew us
the sky took our smoke
the earth our ash
but never our footprint

We remember

their names
we remember
their names
ever upon
our lips
at home
on our tongues
Himmler
Heydrich
Hitler
all so familiar
we remember
Goering
Goebbels
Mengele
and Eichmann
for the rest
see under
German
in most any
book newspaper
or magazine
but who knows
and remembers
wasserman of Baranovitch
zemba of Warsaw
shapiro of Piaseczno
rabbis all
pious to ash
who knows
and remembers
yankel the porter
sosha the washerwoman
velvel the wagoneer
zanvel the sotzialist
esterke the communist
poznanski the kapitalist

malka the fruithandler
shaya the beggar
hinda the rebbe's daughter
szmuel the ragman
leah the mikve lady
mirele the orphan
and the other 231
in the home
unknown
not even forgotten
erased
each and every
unremembered day

Names

once they knew
knew and called
our names
every Sarah
and Avraham
their children
and children's
children's names

Torah names
living scrolls
eaten in fire
parchment flaring
withering ash
letters fluttering
wind driven

fields and forests
trees and fat of the land
orchards and fruit
heavens above
dew below
called us by name
chanting
Rebecca Rachel
Leah Yitzhak
Ya'akov
inscribed
season by season
sow time
harvest
winter death
spring green
Germany knew us
Poland by first name
Ukraine and Lithuania
nameless now

France Holland
doubly muted

above it all
Sinai clouds
ash thick
torrents of names
raining down
ashes and names
earth to earth
dust to dust
ashes to ashes
ashes and names
unknown
uncalled
unwritten

Suffer the little children…

to the ghettoes
Warsaw, Vilne, Lodz, Lublin
Then little children were brought to Jesus
Sara, Rebecca, Leah, Rachel
for him to place his hands on them and pray for them
Avraham, Yitzhak, Ya'akov, Yosef
but the disciples rebuked those who brought them.
Miriam, Yocheved, Tzipora, Elisheva
Jesus said, "Let the little
Barak, Gideon, Shimshon, Shmuel
children come to me,
Yissachar, Zevulon, Gad, Asher
and do not hinder them,
Tirza, Batsheva, Hannah, Penina
for the kingdom of heaven
Auschwitz, Treblinka, Majdanek, Sobibor
belongs to such as these."
Shlomo, Hizkiyahu, Yishayahu, Yirmiyahu
When he had placed his hands on them,
Yentl, Sosha, Mindele, Shprintza
he went on from there.
Belzec, Chelmno, Plaszow, Buchenwald.
And the little children came…

The word become ash

for a while
we lived by the word
I am
you saw no image
I am
the word
unseen and heard
never to become flesh

All the seas ink
All the heavens parchment
Each blade of grass a quill
Each Jew a scribe

we died by the word
before the deed
was done
the word became flesh
and the flesh became ash
we died by the word
just one word
I am
Jude

Beginning with the Crucifixion

and we
thought
alright
he's only
one Jew
let them
have their
just one Jew
appetite satisfied
with just
one Jew
and that'll
be it
just one Jew
and we'll
be saved
and having had one
just one Jew
appetite grew
and grew
for one
more Jew
just another
one more Jew
to save us all
just one Jew
the skulls
grew and grew
of just one more Jew
heaps of skulls
no more Jews
not ever
just one
more Jew

Letter to Paul

i'll forgive you
if you'll forgive me
i'll forgive synagogue
house of the devil
if you'll forgive
jesus not the messiah
i'll forgive yellow
hats and badges
if you'll forgive
flesh of circumcision
i'll forgive some
blood libels
if you'll forgive
keeping the law
i'll forgive children
you took
if you'll forgive
no image at sinai
you'll forgive
i'll forgive
but I
as always
will tell
the tale
to my children
and children's children
lest you forget

From Sinai

in the beginning
it was passed on
it all began when
it was passed on
handed down
from lip to ear
mind to heart
not taught
not instructed
not told
not given
and surely not discussed
it was passed on to us

ere we were
it was
it was passed on to us
and we became
the light
and the law
His flesh
in this life
born again
over and over
after each
and after every
no matter the fire
restoration
the ways of holiness

eat not what they eat
lie not with them and theirs
clothe not thyself as they do
speak not their tongues
be that living passed on Torah

undone erased
you passed it back
in the ovens

Alphabet after six million

We need a new alphabet...
       —Old Jew walking into a gas chamber at Treblinka

A is for ashes aplenty
plenty heaped and heaped
B is for Belzec, Buchenwald
or Bergen Belsen
if you like
where the ashes are heaped aplenty
and of course, Berlin
where it was birthed
C is for...
now what is for C
oh yes
C is for Caroline who did not
ashes to ashes go
Caroline is German
maybe French or even Polish
no ashes to ashes for them
D oh that is easy
ever so easy
D is for David
every Jewboy circumcised David
surely gone to ash
and E that is a tough one
E is for England
who tossed the Jews out
way back when
no Jerusalem builded there
in England's green and pleasant land
F is for Felshtin
a nobody ever heard of Ukrainian village
where all they did
was hack my grandfather
with knives
years before the Germans
manufactured Jew ash

G is for.....? WRONG
not God, too easy
G is for Germans
Especially Goethe
Goering Goebbels and Gropius
and let's not forget Bach Brahms
Beethoven and Schiller
and Heine while we are at it...
oh those Germans
H is for... no, no, no
don't say it...too easy
H is for Hradcany Castle
Yes you got it
Prague so Golden
with civilized Czechs who watched
with mild ever so mild
beer soaked curiosity
I is for nothing
Iceland no Jews there
or ashes for that matter
except volcanic
J is for Jew and ashes all the same
K is for Teutonic Konigsberg
city of oh so
German ethic man Kant
L is for Luther
first among ash making Germans
burn their synagogues and schools
then let's see what's next
M is for mother
all the mothers
of those ashes
N is for Norway
boring little Norway
that managed its own
N is for Nazi regime
O is for

oh dear me
all those Jew ashes
how did they ever
snow all over my
P is for Polish farm fields
Q is for quiet
the central ingredient
for Christian manufacture
and distribution
of Jew ashes
R is for Rotterdam
yes those docile bike riding
tulip head ever so quiet Dutch
easily packaged
and shipped Jews for ashes
S is for Franco Facist Spain who
did not ship and manufacture
Jew ashes
T is for Tiktin
where they just shot the Jews
no ashes there
U is for Uzhgorod
from where they sent my
pious Jews to the ovens
of Auschwitz
ashes all
V is for VE Day
when the ashes
snow flaked all over the continent
W is for this was only
the War Against the Jews
X is for Xavier a saint
whose devoted excelled in ashes
Y is for Yugoslavia where Austrian Waldheim
shot Jews aplenty
but made no ashes
Z is for...

oh I forgot
make it for whatever you like
now I've said
my ABC's...
what have you left for me

I forgot

lest I be...
I should remember
record for all
absent memory
we are not
nor are they

these then I shall remember
as they became
filler and stuffing
in pits wells
crevices ditches ravines
swamps moraines
the quilted topography
here upon the face
of the earth
compost for fertile
Slavic fields

though mostly smoke
and ashes in shades of gray
and hues of black
these I should…

Cezanne's *Nature Morte*

mangos pears
a lemon
pineapple leaves
a skull
two apples
one bitten decaying

memento mori
remember you
will die

amid the birch trees
by the crematoria
on the paths
in the pine breaks
opening to the roaster
by the river Sola
tributary of ashes
still life with Jew

Seeing gazing

whoever sees is seen
whatever is seen sees
capturing face
lip's smile
nose bridge
and hooked
framing jaw
the seen face engraved
frozen imprisoned
on the glanced gazed upon
a thousand years
more or less
we saw
and were seen
day by gazing day
grain fields and orchards
rivers Vistula and Bug
canvases of water
old quarter
market squares
cobbled lanes
muddy roads
but mostly Polish forests vast
oak elm poplar
ash and chestnut
curate our seeing
and seen
gazing faces
in the galleries
an exhibition
portraits of a family
gone to ash wind

Poland's Jews

Lines written in the cemetery of Radomsko, Poland on a spring's snowy day in 1985.

they are there
they really are
everyday
and everywhere

take my hand
see for yourself
they are here
everyday
and everywhere
in this great Polonia of ours
blessed of Madonna
and Virginal blood

he took my hand
they are here
here today
and everyday

where they were
is where they are
in the driving whiting snow
under heaven's earthly skies
gravestones all
large small neat wide
black gray white
lettered etched erased
desecrated faded marred
all shapes sizes
young and old
shivering trembling
in the cold
proud bent broken
huddled

one upon
a shattered other
stonearms
hugging holding
stoneshoulders
leaning lying
weighting another Jew's
broken back
cuddled and huddled
teetering tottering
stone to stone
stone upon stone

stonelife
etched and dated
signed and named
life's walking
ways and deeds
woman's candlesticks
stoneshining
priest's blessing
stonehands
scholar's learning
stonebooks
Levite's laver
stonewater
woman's charity
stonecoins
child's death
stonetree broken
young and old
shivering and trembling
in the cold
proud bent broken
they are here
in this place
of gate's hope abandoned

stonekeeper swings
keys for a zloty
gold or two
to barking dogs'
choral hymns
hell has a native liturgy

beneath blowing snowing
heaven and earth
stones swaying
stones atottering
Jews swaying
shivering and praying
to and fro
everywhere and everyday
in the snowing blowing
angels chanting
dogs barking
they are here
in the air
everywhere
Stonejews

So here is how it goes

I am walking down
wet and muddy stony
really stony alleys
of the Warsaw cemetery
Jewish that is
just by the ghetto
once here and ever
reading those stones
I guess of the lucky
Jew people and persons
who got to die in their beds
at home or hospital
and from the grave beyond
got someone to put up a marker
with all kinds of words
to fix their life in stone
and just across the street
on the now rebuilt Polish city
once lived and then
died killed murdered
some 350,000 Jews
so I along with other
genocide tourists
am looking
for some metaphor or simile
or symbol
that's it symbol
to lend grasp and mastery
even understanding
by which to memorialize
that I was here
isn't that what memory
and metaphor are about
not them the murdered past
but me and us
the here for now
and narcissistic

so this rain is drizzling down on
my 'take a Ralph
once Lifshitz now Lauren cap
it will keep you dry'
this is great
I got me
and us a metaphor
it is drizzling rain
what a God gift
God Himself
crying over it all
that's me metaphor
it works doesn't it
it's raining
God's tears
but they are all
dead and ash

Aleph

The Book of Genesis begins with a Hebrew letter 'b', which in English is rendered as the preposition 'in', as in "In the beginning..." The first letter of the Hebrew alphabet is aleph. The Midrash wonders why the Pentateuch begins with the second letter of the alphabet and not the first. The letter aleph has no sound. It is a silent letter. Thus, the narrative of creation begins not in the beginning but at some point, after the beginning. Before the beginning of the beginning there is ought but chaos and the silent aleph.

when I came not back
just came you know
they asked me
they are always asking
what did you see there
or if you were really there
what did you hear
for one must always see and hear
when one has been somewhere
but I have not been there
and am not really now here
or for that matter anywhere
about which you would
really care to hear
and so I said to they
"there are no colors in
Auschwitz"
they say you lie
oh so many colors
so many hues and shades and shadows
of yellows reds flesh whites
and don't forget black
so many shades
of black
we heard all this they say
but how do you hear a color
there were no colors there
no colors in Auschwitz
no sounds over there

but yes there was one thing
one thing and that is all
and all was in it
God's leftover
from creation Aleph.

Whose pain

the pain of others
is others'
never mine
is the pain
of others
no matter
the pain
it is other
to me
his pain
her pain
their pain
ever other
pogroms
an occasional
expulsion
now and then
and now
a few death camps
the pain of others
is ever other

In search

at mid light
and life
we grope
as the blind
at noon
in the once was
and forgotten
loss and mourning
unearth the buried past
memory makes home
of ruins
nostalgia builds
to emptiness

Auschwitz and Dixie too

But the third rope was still moving; being so light, the child was still alive…for more than half an hour he stayed there struggling between life and death…behind me I heard the same man asking: "Where is God now?" And I heard a voice within me answer him: "Where is He? Here He is—He is hanging here on this gallows…" Night, Elie Wiesel

a tree
of the field
is not a man
not a man
who can flee
and the boy
is not a man
not a man
God hanging
from the tree.

Trees

in Eden
all manner of tree
lustful to the eye
all manner of fruit bearing tree
four rivers watered
each knowing
seed time and harvest
cold and heat
summer and winter
day and night
each in its time
bringing forth
promised land
dates and figs
pomegranates
olives and grapes
as well as
apples beyond Eden
fuji and jonagold
dawn light dew painted
pears bosc and anjou
and a clementine or two for color

all manner of tree
lustful and seed bearing
in Europe and Mississippi
now swing the hanging
fruit of the womb
Jew and Black
on the fruit bearing tree

Epilogue

Tales of old

winter white passing
rainy grey
washed away
turning time and turtle dove
green come into the land
amid the bloody wine
and matza burn
sit a Jew or two
at table candled
against the pagan dark
to tell tales
of old and a few
that are new
about the plagues
of blood lice boils
and don't forget
first born
Egyptian that is
and not Jew
with bloodied doorpost saved
sit a Jew or two
to tell tales of old
and a few that are new
of pillory fires and clouds
of split seas
and broken chariot wheels
and a few promises
as well
we ought remember
the bodies saved
redeemed and consumed
in the fire
that burns the bread
by which we die
even as the winy blood
drains our soul
into the earth

whence it came
and from which
it can still
beyond Eden
cry
to the one
who once said
voice of brother's
winy blood
cries out to me
from the ground
upon which we are
now found
though the mark
be upon us
and our homes
he did not passover
but rather
came in through
the cracks
consuming the walls
and bloodless
Shaddai posts
as matza burn
and wine bloody
bathe
this last Jew supper
and it is
turning time
and spring time
the rain passed
and the turtle dove
cooed in the land
but nary
a Jew voice
declaiming
i too went out from Egypt

Acknowledgments

I was introduced to Jill Baumgaertner by David Heim, immediate past-Editor of *The Christian Century* (the leadership magazine of mainline Protestantism) and a Lutheran minister. Jill Baumgaertner is the Poetry Editor for *The Christian Century*. A much sought-after composer of liturgy, she has published many books of poetry. At our first meeting I mentioned that I had once published a poem or two. She asked to see some of my unpublished poems. She encouraged me to start writing poetry again. She published 12 of my poems in *The Christian Century*. She went through a near forty-year-old thick file of unpublished poems written by me, forgotten, and then found while cleaning out the garage a few years ago. Every single poem in this book is the beneficiary of her wisdom, artistry, poetic craft, and sheer goodness. She spent countless hours with me reviewing each poem and shaping this book. This first small effort of mine would not have come to be without Jill Baumgaertner. These days there are not many American venues for the publication of Jewish theme poetry in the English language. Where else but in America would the poems of an Orthodox rabbi be edited by a traditional Lutheran, who served as Dean of Humanities and Theological Studies at Wheaton College, the Evangelical institution of higher learning, and then published in a mainline Protestant magazine.

I am deeply grateful to David Heim, immediate past Executive Editor and Rev. Peter Marty, current Editor and Publisher of *The Christian Century*, for opening the pages of their fine magazine to my poems.

As I have written, edited, and published poems over the past few years, one person, Mr. Christopher Melton, secured the welfare of my poems through his diligence and technological acumen. Not to speak of the fact that the titles of several poems come from his literary imagination, as do some choice lines that moved several poems out of the paralysis of their first drafts.

Two friends of mine read, commented upon, and improved some of these poems. My thanks to Dr. Alexandra Dunietz, a research scholar in Islam at the University of Chicago.

A great scholar, Dr. David Nirenberg, Dean of the Divinity School at the University of Chicago, read the entire manuscript, made comments which greatly improved some poems, and most significantly, as only an astute historian and reader of classic texts can, described to me the nature of my writing and with whom I was thinking. This I did not realize until he showed me.

I would like to express my heartfelt gratitude to Leah Maines, Kevin Maines, and Christen Kincaid of Finishing Line Press who lent me their wisdom, their expertise, and their kindness, without which this book could not have been published.

In large measure this is a book about loss. To be sure, it is also about memory and continuity. These poems are written that memory bridge the abyss between the silenced storm and life. Continuity is realized in my children and grandchildren, who thankfully did not know those lost worlds. In the Torah itself at critical moments of transition genealogical lists, lists of names are recorded. Life is realized in my children and my children's children.

Yehuda and Nicole Poupko, and their children Shmuel Meir, Ayelet, and Atara;
Elisheva and Kevin Schreiber, and their children Amitai, Erez, and Gadi;
Chaim and Shoshanah Poupko, and their children Ayelet, Elana, and Rachel, and their late sister Chana Tova;
Chaya and Aharon Segal, and their children Sarah, Yonatan, Ariel, Hinda, and Itamar.

Each poem was read and discussed with my most trenchant critic and ardent reader, to whom this book is dedicated.

The following were published on TheLehrhaus.com, September 18, 2020.

This is not a poem
Starlings and pigeons
Kol Nidrei—All my vows
Roster
When the goat escaped

Author Biography

Rabbi **Yehiel E. Poupko** is Rabbinic Scholar at the Jewish Federation of Metropolitan Chicago. He is responsible for the Jewish community's interfaith relations with a variety of local, national, and international Protestant, Evangelical, and Catholic seminaries, churches, institutions, and leaders. He is the author of *Chana: A Life in Prayer*, the first full length treatment of the drama of Hannah in the Bible and its reception in Rabbinic literature and liturgy. His poetry has been published in *The Christian Century*. He is the author of the scholarly introduction to the classic Rabbinic work, *Pesikta De Rav Kahana*.

www.ingramcontent.com/pod-product-compliance
Lightning Source LLC
Chambersburg PA
CBHW021157090426
42740CB00008B/1124